(Focus on...)

THE ... OF
BENELUX

ED NEEDHAM

FRANKLIN WATTS
LONDON · SYDNEY

This edition printed in 2004

© Aladdin Books Ltd 1994

ISBN 0-7496-5479-1

A CIP catalogue record for this book is available from the British Library.

Printed in U.A.E.

Designer	Flick Book Design and Graphics.
Series director	Bibby Whittaker
Editors	Jim Pipe
	Mark Jackson
Picture Research	Brooks Krikler Research
Illustrator	Dave Burroughs

The author, Ed Needham, has travelled extensively in Europe and has published several books on European countries.

The consultant, Henk Bakker, was born in the Netherlands and has a degree in philosophy. He now lives and works in Britain.

INTRODUCTION

The Benelux countries – Belgium, the Netherlands and Luxembourg – lie at the heart of northern Europe. Despite a history of repeated invasion by foreign powers, they have each retained a unique culture and together maintain a global importance far in excess of their size. The landscape, from the flat Dutch polders to the wooded mountains of the Ardennes, is as varied as the people who inhabit it. This book offers an insight into the Benelux countries and peoples, combining related information from the fields of geography, language and literature, science and maths, history and the arts. The key below shows how the subjects are divided up.

Geography
The symbol of the planet Earth shows where geographical facts and activities are to be found. These sections include a look at the beautiful Ardennes region and the techniques used to reclaim land from the sea.

Language and literature
An open book is the sign for activities which involve language and literature. One such panel looks at Dutch words which have come into common use in English, while another explores the language frontier in Belgium. A further panel highlights the two famous Belgian authors Hergé and Georges Simenon.

Science and maths
The microscope symbol indicates where a science project or science information is given. If the symbol is tinted green, it signals an environmental issue. One panel looks at the Dutch approach to the environment.

History
The sign of the scroll and hourglass shows where historical information is given. These sections look at key events in the history of the Benelux countries and their impact on society.

Social history
The symbol of the family indicates where information about social history is given. Descriptions of rural and city life create a flavour of Benelux today.

Arts, crafts and music
The symbol showing a sheet of music and artist's tools signals arts, crafts or musical activities. Topics covered in this category include the Luxembourg-born botanical artist Redouté, the inventor of the saxophone and a project to build a model windmill.

CONTENTS

THE BENELUX COUNTRIES

Belgium, the Netherlands and Luxembourg are small, densely populated nations in north-western Europe, collectively known as the Benelux countries (the Benelux flag is on the left). For centuries, these countries were ruled by the same foreign powers but, since gaining independence, they have played an important role in Europe and as colonial powers in countries such as the Congo and Indonesia. Over the last fifty years, they have banded together economically to exploit their position at "the crossroads of Europe".

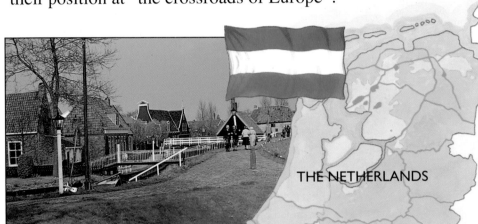

THE NETHERLANDS

BELGIUM

LUXEMBOURG

Luxembourg
The Grand Duchy of Luxembourg covers just 2,586 square kilometres and has a population of around 454,000. Osling, the northern region, is wooded and hilly, while Gutland, in the south, is flatter. As a tax haven, Luxembourg (below) is also a major centre for commerce and banking.

The Netherlands
The Kingdom of the Netherlands is often mistakenly called Holland, which in fact is only a region within the country. The Kingdom occupies 33,938 square kilometres, and has a population of over 16.2 million. The word Netherlands means "low countries" – it is mostly flat, with much of the land below sea level.

Belgium
The Kingdom of Belgium covers 30,528 square kilometres and has a population of over 10 million. It is often described as being the shape of a bunch of grapes. Like the Netherlands, much of Belgium is low-lying and linked by a complex system of canals. The Ardennes region, in the south-east, is more mountainous. The capital Brussels (the Grand Place is shown left) is both a major commercial and industrial centre and home to the European Parliament.

Population pressure

The Benelux countries are among the most densely populated areas in the world. The Netherlands averages 463 people per square kilometre, compared to 240 per square kilometre in the UK and just 27 per square kilometre in North America. This tends to mean busy streets, crowded roads and very few large areas of open land without any buildings. In all three countries, the vast majority of the population is urban.

Place in Europe

The Benelux countries form a wedge in north-western Europe with the North Sea to the west, north Germany to the east and France to the south-west. Britain is a short journey across the North Sea. They have long exploited their position by building their prosperity on trade with these three large neighbours.

Language frontiers

The Benelux countries are a patchwork of language groups. In the Netherlands, people speak Dutch, except in Friesland, where they speak Frisian. Luxembourg has its own language, Letzeburgesch, though French and German are official languages too. Belgium is split into Flanders, where they speak Flemish (a form of Dutch), and Wallonia, where they speak French. A minority speak German.

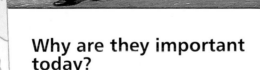

Why are they important today?

After the Second World War, Belgium, the Netherlands and Luxembourg formed the Benelux Customs Union. This made trade easier between them, and helped them to operate as a stronger block in competition with larger nations. They made up three of the six countries to sign the Treaty of Rome in 1957, which brought the Common Market into being. This has since developed into the European Union.

NETHERLANDS

Flanders

Brussels

Wallonia

BELGIUM

- Fr/Flemish
- German
- Dutch
- French

LUXEMBOURG

EARLY HISTORY

The flat countryside has made the region easy for foreign powers to invade. The Romans arrived in 58 BC, led by Julius Caesar, conquering all the land up to the Rhine. During the 14th century, the French house of Burgundy and then the Austrian house of Hapsburg took control, both attracted by the area's prosperity. In the 16th century, Protestantism reached the northern provinces (the modern Netherlands), which split away, while Belgium and Luxembourg remained under the Catholic Spaniards.

Date chart

4,000 BC	Region settled by Celts. (A Celtic bracelet is shown at the top of the page.)
58 BC-400 AD	Belgium and some of the Netherlands under Roman rule.
481-843	Franks control the region.
768	Pope declares the Frankish king Charlemagne (left) Emperor of the West.
10th century	Independent duchies, counties and towns established. Cloth trade makes the area prosperous. Start of the use of waterways.
14th-15th centuries	French dukes of Burgundy take control and unite the area.
1477	Through a marriage alliance, the Low Countries (a term referring to what are now the Benelux countries) pass to the Austrian Hapsburg family.
1516	The Low Countries become a Spanish possession, under Charles V.
1566	Revolt of the Netherlands begins. Protestants become fed up with harsh Spanish rule of Philip II. Revolt led by William the Silent, Prince of Orange.
1581	The Dutch declare their independence from Spain. Belgium and Luxembourg remain Catholic and under Spanish control.
17th century	The Netherlands becomes world's leading sea power.
1648	Spain finally recognises Dutch independence.

A Peasant Wedding – instead of the biblical scenes favoured by his contemporaries, Pieter Brueghel the Elder (1520-69) painted pictures of ordinary people, showing how they lived and how towns and villages looked in the 16th century.

Cloth guilds

In the Middle Ages, the clothworking trade made cities like Ghent and Bruges among the richest in Europe. Feudal lords gave charters to merchant guilds. These gave the merchants special privileges and made them rich and powerful. To join a guild, it was necessary to serve an apprenticeship of several years, and no one could trade without belonging to the guild.

Belgae tribe

"Of all the people of Gaul," said Julius Caesar, "the Belgae are the bravest". The Romans defeated this Celtic tribe in 57 BC, and called the area Belgica. In the 3rd century AD, Belgium was divided between Germans in the north and Celts in the south – the origin of its language split.

Burgundians and Hapsburgs

Prior to the 11th century, foreign rulers took little interest in the Low Countries. But when thriving fishing, shipping and textile industries developed, the French dukes of Burgundy were quick to take control. They achieved this by a combination of inheritance, marriage, money and war. Under the Burgundians, trade and the arts continued to flourish in the region. Through marriage, authority passed to the Austrian Hapsburgs in 1477, but in 1506 the region came under Charles V, King of Spain, who was born in Ghent. People said his empire was so vast that the sun never set on it. When the Netherlands split off, Belgium and Luxembourg remained Hapsburg dominions until Napoleon invaded in 1795.

When Mary of Burgundy (left) married Maximilian I in 1477, the Low Countries came under Hapsburg control.

William the Silent

William, Prince of Orange, was a moderate man who was horrified by the brutal Spanish regime of Philip II. He led the Revolt of the Netherlands, which began in 1566.

Reformation era

The Reformation was a 16th-century movement to reform the Church. Many felt that the Catholic Church had grown corrupt, and preferred the austere Protestant beliefs of Martin Luther and John Calvin. The Spanish considered themselves defenders of the Catholic faith, and were incensed by the spread of Protestantism. Charles V's son King Philip II (right) tortured, imprisoned and executed Protestants to try and control them. But the Dutch grew rich, despite long wars against the Spanish, and they achieved full independence in 1648.

INDEPENDENCE ONWARDS

The Dutch Golden Age came to an end in 1714, a year after Belgium and Luxembourg passed from Spanish back to Austrian control. At the end of the century, all three countries were conquered by Napoléon (left), and after his fall they were grouped together as the Kingdom of the Netherlands, until Belgium and Luxembourg won their independence in 1830. After the destruction of two world wars, the three countries formed the Benelux Customs Union in 1947, to give them a better trading position.

Waterloo
Waterloo, a town near Brussels, saw Napoléon's final defeat in 1815. After returning from exile on Elba, he fought on for a hundred days, until defeated by an army under Wellington.

Leopold I
Leopold I became the first King of the Belgians in 1831. Despite constant friction between Walloons and Flemings, Leopold's diplomacy held together the fledgling country, which powerful neighbours threatened to devour.

A colonial past
The Netherlands colonised Indonesia and Surinam in the 17th century. Indonesia was the base for the Dutch East India Company's trade with the Orient. The Dutch captured the Caribbean islands of Aruba and Antilles from the Spanish in 1634, plus land around New York (then called New Amsterdam). Dutch settlers also founded the Cape colony in 1652 – the Afrikaaners are their descendants. In the 19th century, Belgium colonised the African countries of Congo, Rwanda and Burundi.

A bridge too far
One of the most daring actions of the Second World War took place in the Netherlands, when 35,000 troops were dropped near the town of Arnhem in an attempt to capture the bridge over the Rhine. But the plan failed due to poor intelligence and many paratroopers died needlessly.

Wartime heroines

Anne Frank (1929-45) was a German Jew whose family fled to Amsterdam to escape the Nazis in 1933. During Nazi occupation of the Netherlands, they hid in a secret room until they were betrayed. Anne died in Belsen concentration camp. Her diary was published in 1947 and made into a film. Queen Wilhelmina of the Netherlands (1880-1962) won the admiration of her people during the war because of her constant encouragement of the Dutch resistance.

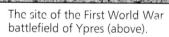

The site of the First World War battlefield of Ypres (above).

Modern-day Luxembourgers celebrate the gaining of independence in 1830.

Date chart

1652-74	The Netherlands fight three naval wars with England to keep control of the seas.
1701-14	The Dutch lose control of the seas to England, following war with France.
1713	Following the War of the Spanish Succession, Luxembourg and Belgium return to the Austrian Hapsburgs.
1795	Napoléon invades. The Netherlands becomes the Batavian Republic, and Belgium and Luxembourg are annexed to France.
1815	The Congress of Vienna joins the three countries in the Kingdom of the Netherlands.
1830	Belgium and Luxembourg declare their independence.
1914-18	Belgium fights against Germany in the First World War and suffers terrible destruction. The Netherlands remains neutral.
1940-45	Germany occupies the Benelux countries during the Second World War.
1957	The three countries help establish the European Common Market.
1971	Belgian constitution divides country into three communities based on language.
1980	Belgian Parliament grants partial autonomy to Flanders and Wallonia.
1992	Belgium, Luxembourg and the Netherlands sign the Maastricht Treaty.
2002	Belgium, Luxembourg and the Netherlands join the European single currency.

The Atomium

The Atomium stands in the Exhibition Park in Brussels, and has become a symbol of the city. It is an aluminium model of a carbon molecule magnified 165 billion times, and it was built for the 1958 World's Fair. It was designed by the Belgian architect Eugene Waterkeyn. The spheres are connected by escalators.

At its highest point, the Atomium (right) is 120m above ground.

BELGIAN CITIES

As many as 97 per cent of Belgians live in towns or cities. Brussels is the largest Belgian city and, together with its suburbs, is the only one with a population of over a million. Brussels is bilingual and claims to be the capital of Europe, with the European Parliament and hundreds of international companies and organisations located there. Belgian towns (a typical town square is shown above left) are linked by the world's densest railway network, and by motorways that emanate from Brussels like spokes, which are easily identifiable from the air.

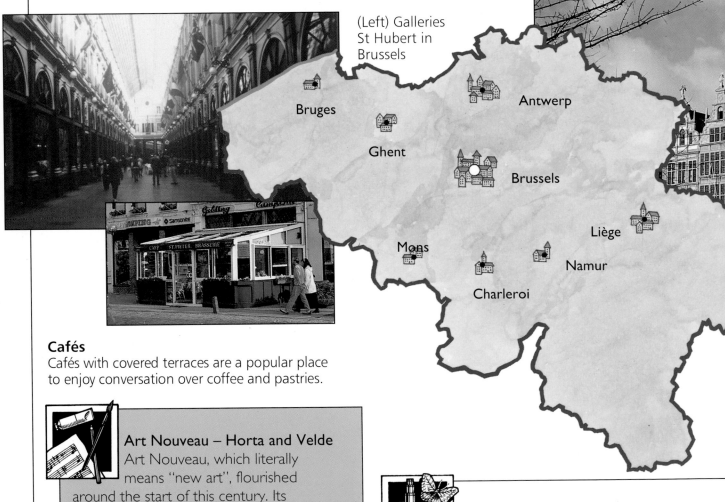

(Left) Galleries St Hubert in Brussels

Bruges

Ghent

Antwerp

Brussels

Mons

Charleroi

Liège

Namur

Cafés
Cafés with covered terraces are a popular place to enjoy conversation over coffee and pastries.

Art Nouveau – Horta and Velde
Art Nouveau, which literally means "new art", flourished around the start of this century. Its characteristic plant and flower patterns and elegant curling lines became fashionable in architecture and the decorative arts. Baron Victor Horta (1861-1947), a Belgian architect, was one of the originators of Art Nouveau, as was Henri Clemens van de Velde (1863-1957), who designed furniture, ceramics, metalwork (right) and textiles.

Belgian chocolates
Belgian chocolates by manufacturers such as Godiva, Neuhaus and Gartner are famous the world over for their quality. One reason why Belgian chocolates taste so good is because of the high percentage of milk fats used. One of the qualities of milk fats is that they melt just below body temperature, making them melt as soon as you put them in your mouth!

Antwerp

Antwerp, the largest city in Flanders, was once the hub of an international trading empire. With the decline of Bruges in the late 15th century, Europe's great trading families moved to Antwerp. Its Golden Age lasted less than 100 years, and the city declined until Napoléon revived its docks as "a pistol pointed at the heart of England". Today, it is the centre of the world's diamond trade.

The Money Lender and his Wife (above). This painting by Massys (c.1466-1530) illustrates Belgium's long association with gold and precious stones – Bruges was Europe's first money exchange.

Antwerp's central square (left)

Ghent and Bruges

Bruges was the capital of medieval Flanders, and was Europe's chief wool-manufacturing town and market. It is one of the best-preserved medieval cities in Europe, and takes its name from the word for "bridge", after the bridges over its canals. Ghent remains a major centre for textiles and lacemaking.

Belgian constitution

Belgium is a parliamentary democracy, governed by rules first established by the 1830 constitution. The king is the head of state. Since 1970 some powers have been given up by central government. The Flemish, French-speaking and German-speaking communities are responsible for education and cultural affairs. The Flanders, Wallonia and Brussels regions are responsible for public works, transport and some social, economic and administrative matters.

BELGIAN COUNTRYSIDE

The Belgian countryside varies greatly. The north is similar to the Netherlands: flat and laced with canals and river deltas. To the south-east are the mountains and woodlands of the Ardennes. Elsewhere there are rolling fields. Agriculture accounts for only two per cent of the workforce, but occupies nearly half the country's surface area, and produces most of the country's food requirements. The temperate climate and fertile soil provide ideal conditions for growing foodstuffs, horticulture and raising livestock. Belgium's most important rivers are the Scheldt, Sambre and Meuse.

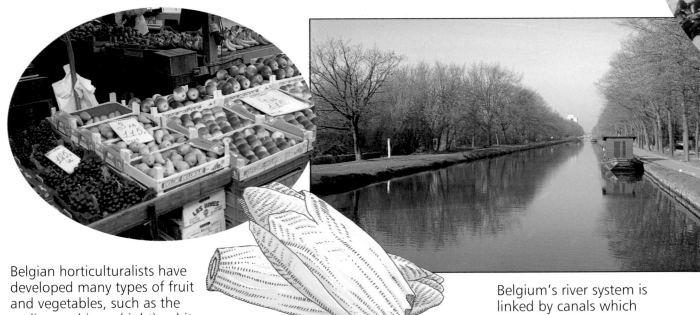

Belgian horticulturalists have developed many types of fruit and vegetables, such as the endive or chicory (right), white asparagus, Conference pears (above left) and the Brussels sprout (top of page).

Belgium's river system is linked by canals which are ideal for carrying bulky goods that do not need to travel quickly.

Coastline
Belgium's only natural frontier is its 63km of North Sea coastline, most of which has wide, sandy beaches. Fishermen catch shrimps by the traditional method of dragging heavy nets on horseback through the shallow water. Mussels (left) are another very popular seafood in Belgium.

What's in a face?
The painter Frans Hals (1583-1666) was born in Antwerp but spent most of his life in Haarlem in the Netherlands. He is best known for his ability to capture expressions on the faces of his subjects.
Look at the painting *A Family Group* (right). How do you think the artist has conveyed the subjects' feelings towards each other?

Fish and seafood, such as crab and lobster, are popular in Belgium. Cockles and eels are considered special delicacies.

Spiere
Spiere - Helkijn
Espierres
Espierres - Helchin

Walloons and Flemings

Belgium is divided by the 1,500 year-old "language frontier" that splits the country into French and Dutch-speaking regions, and affects all areas of Belgian life from road signs (left) to posters (below). During the 19th century, the French-speaking Walloons were dominant, as Belgian industry was concentrated in the south. As the steel industry declined, the majority Flemish population became more influential.

De BBL-Kaart 12/15 — JOEPIE, IK BEN ER 12! — De BBL denkt aan u...

La Carte BBL 12/15 — ENFIN 12 ANS! — La BBL pense à vous...

The Ardennes

The Ardennes region in the south-east has some of Europe's most spectacular scenery. The Ardennes is Belgium's least populated area and has little agriculture, apart from some good grazing land. Its densely wooded valleys are home to a large variety of wildlife, such as wild boar, wild cats, deer (below) and pheasant. The Ardennes is particularly popular with hill-walkers, as the mountains are not especially high but boast wonderful views. The area is also popular with skiers in the winter months. Mount Botrange, at 694m, is the highest point in Belgium. Many local springs produce mineral-rich water which is bottled and exported. The town of Spa in the Ardennes has given its name to all towns with health-giving springs.

Agricultural produce

Belgian farmers grow both modern and traditional crops. One of the oldest crops is flax, which produces linseed oil, the traditional ingredient of paints. The long fibres that form the stem of the flax plant can be woven into linen, a very strong cloth. Belgium is the world's largest producer of azaleas and is Europe's largest exporter of Christmas trees. Belgian farmers also export large quantities of sugar beet and potatoes.

BELGIAN LEISURE

The Belgians have a reputation for working hard and taking life seriously. The average working week is 38-39 hours, and most people have four weeks' holiday per year. In their spare time, Belgians enjoy sports such as soccer, and during the year there are also many carnivals and processions. Education is very important in Belgium. Students spend more time at school than in almost any other country, and 25 per cent of them go on to university. As Belgium is a small country surrounded by others, Belgians can easily pick up television programmes from France, Germany and Britain.

Sign for a cycle route

Education
Education is compulsory between the ages of 6 and 18, and is always in the language of the community. Belgium has two school systems: official schools, which are run by the government, and free schools, which are normally run by the Catholic Church.

Bicycles
Bicycles are the ideal form of transport in a flat country, and cycling is very popular as a sport too. The Belgian Eddy Merckx, nicknamed "The Cannibal", won the Tour de France a record-equalling five times.

Maigret meets Tintin
Two of the world's most published authors are Belgian, and both created famous detectives. Georges Simenon (1903-89) wrote about the pipe-smoking Jules Maigret, and Hergé (1907-83) invented Tintin, the journalist turned sleuth. Simenon published over 500 novels, while Hergé published only 24 Tintin stories, although their works have since been translated into dozens of languages and sold over 100 million copies. Hergé took his name by reversing (the sounds of) the French initials of his real name, Georges Remi.

Sports and leisure

Belgians are very keen on sport, although many prefer to watch it rather than participate. Cycling and football (below left) are the most popular spectator sports. On Sunday afternoons, cycle races often take place in the streets of provincial towns. One of the stranger sports is pigeon racing (above left), where pigeons are taken to a distant part of the country and have to find their way home as fast as possible. Hunting and fishing are popular, as are walking and camping in the hills of the Ardennes.

Eating out

Many Belgians prefer their own company and that of close friends, and like to keep their home life private. Rather than invite friends to visit, they prefer to go out in the evening (see above) and enjoy a meal at a restaurant. Most Belgians are very fond of their food!

Adolphe Sax (1814-94)

Born in Dinant, Sax is best known for inventing the saxophone (right) in about 1840. He also produced other brass instruments, such as the saxhorn and the saxtuba.

Festivals and carnival

Belgium has many different festivals – the origins of some are so old that they have been forgotten. Carnival is held just before Lent, a last celebration before 40 days of abstinence. At Mons, there is a re-enactment of St George's battle with the dragon. For 500 years, the clowns of Binche (right) have paraded with ostrich feathers to mark the arrival of the first South American Indians in Europe. At Ypres, in the Festival of the Cats, model cats and witches are thrown into the crowd. There are also Belgian festivals to celebrate the harvest.

Cooking beef carbonnade

A carbonnade used to mean a dish that was grilled or boiled over the coals, but now means a stew. It is a typically Flemish meal. Try this recipe for yourself:

First, cut 675g of chuck steak into squares and brown it in 125g of butter. Then remove the meat and soften 450g of chopped onions in the butter. Place the meat and onions in a heavy pan. Add 330ml of beer and some beef stock. Stir some flour into the fat remaining in the pan, together with a little more stock (you need about 330ml of stock in total), and stir until it thickens.

Finally, add the mixture to the meat, season with a tablespoon of brown sugar, salt and pepper. Cover and cook gently for two hours, et voilà!, a delicious meal for four.

BELGIAN RESOURCES

Belgium was swift to industrialise, yet today its prosperity is based on services, which employ over 70 per cent of the workforce. Its location has made it a major trading nation, and it is heavily dependent on international trade as it has few natural resources of its own. Almost two-thirds of all economic activity takes place in Flanders. The most important industries are metallurgy, machine and motor construction, food and chemicals.

Import – export
International trade is so important to the Belgian economy that one Belgian in two works for the export industry, and more than 50 per cent of national production is exported. Belgium imports raw materials, like iron ore, and exports finished or semi-finished products, such as steel and machinery. Belgium's steel industry used to be based near the coalfields in Wallonia. These mines are now exhausted, and today the industry is oil-powered, so the steel plants have been moved to Flanders near the oil ports. This move shifted the power balance between Walloons and Flemings.

Though in the past the Belgian economy relied heavily on its steel industry, today's diverse economy is a combination of high quality technology and traditional craftsmanship, producing everything from lasers and modern synthetic fibres to lace and crystal glass.

Diamond cutting

A Belgian master cutter may examine an uncut diamond for weeks before cutting it. The rough diamond is held in a "dop" or shell. An incision is made, and the diamond is then expertly split (below left). To create each facet, the tiny surfaces that make diamonds sparkle, the stone is held against a diamond dusted disc at a precise angle (below right).

Antwerp port
Antwerp (above right) on the river Scheldt, is 88km from the sea, but it is still Europe's second largest port. It became a major port in the 15th century, when the larger port at Bruges became blocked by storms. By the early 16th century, Antwerp was full of foreign businesses dealing with the rest of Europe. Water transport is still vital to Belgium's economy, with more than 2,000km of inland waterways. Antwerp handles over 20,000 ships each year, from over 800 other ports, and claims to be the fastest in the world at unloading and reloading ships.

The appealing design and bright colours of these old Gevaert film boxes made them easily identifiable.

A photographic pioneer

Lieven Gevaert (1868-1935) was a pioneer in the field of photography, especially in producing photographic materials. Born in Antwerp, he combined his skills as an inventor and businessman to improve the quality of photography and make it accessible to more people.

Euros (right)

Belgian scientists

Abbé Lemaître (1894-1966), an astrophysicist and priest, developed the Big Bang theory to explain the origin of the universe. He believed that all matter was once condensed in an unimaginably dense state, and has been expanding ever since. Etienne Lenoir (1822-1900) invented the first practical internal combustion gas engine (below). Leo Baekeland (1863-1944) emigrated to the USA, where he invented Bakelite, a forerunner of modern plastics.

Holy beers

The Belgians have long been great brewers, and today produce hundreds of different brands of beer. The recipes are often several hundred years old, and are well-kept secrets. In the Middle Ages, breweries were often run by monks. The abbeys encouraged the science of brewing, and introduced hops to flavour the beer.

Lacemaking

Belgian lace, made from linen or cotton, has been prized for centuries. Made by twisting and braiding bobbins, it originated in Flanders in the 16th century and requires great craftsmanship and patience to make. By 1600, it was a luxury product worn by men and women. With the invention of a machine that copied handmade lace around 1840, prices fell, and demand increased dramatically. From 1850 to 1914 an estimated 20,000 lacemakers were based in the towns of Bruges, Ghent and Brussels. Today, hand-made lace is largely sold as a souvenir item.

DUTCH CITIES

The Netherlands is one of world's most densely populated countries. Most of the population is concentrated in the Randstad, a conurbation in the west of the country, where most of the industry is also located. Each of the four major cities, all within the Randstad, have a population of over 200,000. Though the population is growing, a strong Dutch reaction to tower blocks has led to a synthesis of old and new architecture (see the traditional bridge, above left, and modern housing, below centre). The Dutch capital is Amsterdam, but its seat of government is in The Hague.

Amsterdam
Many of Amsterdam's streets are waterways lined with 17th-century houses, earning it the nickname "the Venice of the North". It is an important cultural centre with many famous museums, a rich nightlife, characterful bars and a notorious red-light area.

A bustling street in Amsterdam reveals the contrast of old buildings and modern city life.

Double Dutch?
A few Dutch words have made the leap into the English language such as brandy, skate, skipper and yacht. The word "yankee", used to describe people from the northern states of the United States, may have begun as a nickname for Dutch colonists who arrived there. Cookie comes from the Dutch *koekje*.

Religious differences
For centuries, religion played a key part in the division of Dutch society. Since the Second World War, these divisions (known as *verzuiling*) have faded, but even today, being a Protestant or Catholic can influence one's choice of newspaper, political party, school or hospital. While Catholics represent just over 30 per cent of the population, and Protestants just over 20 per cent, an even larger percentage of the Dutch now claim no religious affiliation.

Traditional architecture

Amsterdam's elegant *gracht* houses (right) are deliberately narrow. Rich merchants demanded that their houses had access to the gracht (which provided drinking water), so the gable-fronted houses were tightly packed to make the most of the limited space. Even so, there is plenty of room inside, as the houses run a long way back. Amsterdam lies on marshy ground, so deep piles have to be driven to provide solid foundations.

Amsterdam's *grachtengordel* canal network was created in the 17th century to cater for a wealthier, expanding population. The three main canals are all over 3km long and in the shape of a crescent. Today, the canal system provides a pleasant contrast to busy roads clogged with cars.

Street art

Dutch cities house many famous art museums, and the country has a long artistic tradition, although street art has few links in common with the past. While many consider such urban decorations colourful and inspired, others prefer their art to be more conventional. In busy cities, cycles are often painted in individual ways in an attempt to deter bicycle thieves.

Mata Hari, secret agent:

Mata Hari was the stage name of Margarethe Geertruida Zelle (1876-1917), a Dutch dancer. During the First World War, she seduced many high-ranking officials and leaked Allied secrets to the Germans. She may have been a double agent for both France and Germany, but was eventually shot by the French for espionage.

DUTCH COUNTRYSIDE

Fewer than four per cent of the Dutch population work in agriculture and fishing, although half the land in the Netherlands is under cultivation and provides large surpluses for export. Agriculture ranges from bulb growing (above) and dairy farms to the fruit farms of the Gelderland province. Half of the Netherlands is below sea level, and much of the land reclaimed from the sea. The provinces are made up partly of intensively farmed countryside, where people live in modest gabled houses, and partly in garden suburbs, where new towns lie in the midst of rape fields and the inhabitants commute to the big cities.

Profits in the fishing industry (below) have fallen over recent years as overfishing has reduced stocks. Dutch fishermen trawl for herring, mackerel and cod in the North Sea. In the Irish Sea, they fish for flat fish, such as plaice and sole, with boats called cutters, and in Danish and German waters they fish for shrimp. Shellfish are caught in the Eastern Scheldt and the Waddenzee.

Polders

Sand Plains

Dunes

Southern Uplands

Friesian cows (above) are famous for their creamy milk.

Strange pastimes
A number of unusual pastimes are found in the Netherlands, and especially in Friesland. One of these is the *Elfstedentocht*, a 125km skating race over the frozen canals linking 11 towns. As many as 18,000 competitors take part. Pole vaulting over dykes is called *fierljeppen*, and competitors who don't make it get a drenching. *Wadlopen*, or walking over mudflats at low tide, is also popular in the summer months.

Land reclamation
The Dutch have reclaimed so much land from the sea that, according to an old saying, "God created the world, but the Dutch created Holland". Dutch history is tied to the struggle against the sea, and since the Middle Ages they have been reclaiming land by building dykes, or raised earth banks, around a lake. Water used to be pumped from the lake into a canal by windmills – this is now done by diesel pumps. The land that is left is called a polder (right), and is often very fertile. In the 1930s, the 30km Barrier Dam was built across the Zuider Zee, creating the new province of Flevoland and the IJsselmeer lake.

Windmills

To make a model windmill, take two pieces of thin card (4cm x 8cm). Fold them lengthways, so that one side overlaps the other. Push the overlapping edges together and tape them together, so one side is curved. Glue them to a straw, with the curved face up (see diagram), and tape another straw at right angles, to use as a spindle. Push this through a hole in an old drinks carton (see diagram).

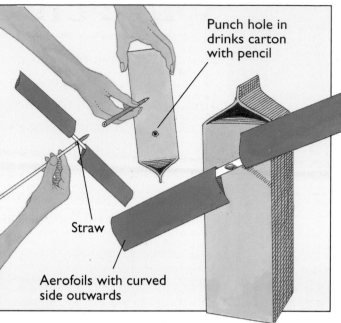

Punch hole in drinks carton with pencil

Straw

Aerofoils with curved side outwards

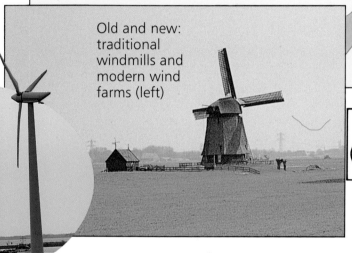

Old and new: traditional windmills and modern wind farms (left)

Different regions

The Netherlands has four main land regions: the Dunes, which curve around the North Sea coast; the Polders; the Sand Plains, a rolling agricultural and forested area; and the Southern Uplands, around Maastricht.

Cheese

The Dutch cheese Gouda is sold in four forms, as bacteria in the cheese causes it to change with age. *Jong* is a creamy cheese, *belegen* is four months old, *oud* is 10 months old, while *overbelegen* is a crumbly old cheese. Edam, with its famous red paraffin coat, was originally brushed with vermilion to distinguish it from other cheeses.

Dyke   Reclaimed land   Dyke   Sea

Regional dress and clogs

Many of the simple and practical Dutch traditional costumes are still worn in rural areas. Zeeland, once inhabited by farmers and merchants, has the most sumptuous costumes, as the skippers brought back expensive materials from abroad. A million *klompen*, or clogs, are sold every year to Friesians, who wear them as everyday shoes. These clogs are light and strong, unlike those in souvenir shops (right).

DUTCH LEISURE

Approximately one-third of the Dutch population are members of sports clubs. Soccer, hockey, tennis and sailing are all popular, and many people skate on the frozen canals during the winter. Since the 17th century, Dutch artists from Rembrandt (left) to Van Gogh have exhibited a distinctive national character in their paintings. Education is very important in the Netherlands, and the roots of the education system can be traced back to the Batavian Republic, the state established in the Low Countries by Napoléon.

Education

Students begin secondary school at 11. There are many different types of secondary school, which help train students for jobs, or prepare them for university. Leiden University, which was founded in 1575, is the oldest and most renowned in the Netherlands.

Education is compulsory in the Netherlands between the ages of 5 and 16, although it is possible to start school at 4.

Food

Dutch food is traditionally simple and wholesome, with different breads, plenty of vegetables, meat and fish, and lots of dairy produce. Warming dishes like *hutspot* (carrots, onions and potatoes mashed together) are especially good for bitter winters. Herrings are another speciality, traditionally eaten by holding the tail and dropping them into the mouth (left).

Environmental concerns

The Dutch are a very environmentally-conscious nation, and the headquarters of Greenpeace, the international campaigning organisation, is in Amsterdam. A programme launched in 1990, with the slogan "A better environment starts with you", spread the message that everybody could help. It encouraged people to buy environmentally friendly products, to separate kitchen and garden waste from household waste, and use a bicycle instead of the car. There are now over 11 million bicycles (above) in the Netherlands. Some people even move house by means of an old-fashioned *bakfiets* or baker's bicycle!

Sport

Football is the most popular sport in the Netherlands. The Dutch international side is renowned for attacking, imaginative football, and has produced many great players, such as Johan Cruyff "the Flying Dutchman", Ruud Gullit (below), famous for his dreadlocked headers, and Ruud Van Nistelrooy. Athletics, swimming, cycling and tennis are all popular, as are water sports like sailing (above).

Walking events such as the Nijmegen marathon are highly organised, but are as much communal activities as competitive sports.

In some towns in Zeeland, *krulbollen*, a form of bowling, is played, while in Friesland there are *skutjeslien*, races in flat-bottomed sailing boats.

Royal family

Crowned in 1980, Queen Beatrix is the head of state of the Netherlands, Aruba and the Antilles. The monarchy is extremely popular, partly because the House of Orange was closely linked to the struggle for independence, and partly because the modern royal family are regarded as being very down-to-earth – the Dutch people tend to mock any *camponses* (self-importance).

The Dutch masters

The Netherlands has produced an astonishing number of world-class artists for such a small nation. The works of Dutch 16th- and 17th-century masters, such as Hieronymous Bosch, Rembrandt, Hals and Vermeer (his painting *The Lacemaker* is shown below left), command fortunes on the international art market. In the 19th and 20th centuries, artists like Van Gogh (1853-90) and Mondrian broke new ground artistically, although it wasn't always recognised during their lifetimes. Vincent Van Gogh's *Sunflowers* is among the world's most famous pictures, but Vincent sold only one painting during his lifetime – to his brother – and killed himself at the scene of his last work. Below right is Van Gogh's painting *The Lilac Bush*.

DUTCH RESOURCES

The Netherlands has exploited its location in Europe to become a major trading nation. Standing at the mouths of the Rhine, Maas and Waal rivers, the country plays a leading part in world trade, and Rotterdam is the world's busiest port. Major industries are food, alcohol, tobacco, chemicals, oil refining and metallurgy. The Netherlands is also Europe's largest supplier of natural gas. Today, famous firms such as Akzo, Unilever, Shell and Philips (a respected electronics innovator) fly the Dutch flag abroad.

Energy

The Netherlands is Europe's largest producer and supplier of natural gas, most of which comes from the North Sea. Approximately 95 per cent of homes are connected to the gas network, and it is also used to generate electricity. The Netherlands produces some of its own oil, but the refineries at Rotterdam use oil brought from around the world. The government promotes a variety of energy-saving campaigns and also invests in the search for alternative energy sources, such as wind power (see wind farms on p. 21).

Two young Dutch aviators set up firms in 1919 – Albert Plesman, who founded KLM, the Royal Dutch Airlines (above), and Anthony Fokker, whose company went on to provide instruments for both the Giotto space probe and the Ariane rocket programme. Two Anglo-Dutch industrial giants are Shell (left), a petroleum and agrochemicals company, and Unilever, makers of soaps and washing powders.

Euros

Waterways

The Netherlands' 4,339km of navigable canals and waterways carry goods deep into the European mainland, or ship them out for export around the world. Rotterdam (centre of spread) is accessible to the world's largest tankers, and is also the port with the largest turnover (over 300 million tonnes of goods a year) in the world. Of all the goods loaded or unloaded in the European Union (EU), 30 per cent pass through Dutch ports. Dutch carriers perform about half of all water trade in the EU, and the Netherlands has more rivercraft than any other country. Canals also help drain the country's low-lying land, and boost tourism as they are an attractive part of the landscape.

Dutch canals are a great way for tourists to get around.

Delftware

Delft, in the western Netherlands, is famous for its distinctive porcelain (a mixture of clays which becomes translucent when fired). Though the town had produced pottery for many years, when traders brought porcelain back from China in the early 1600s, potters started to copy the blue and white designs. By the mid-17th century there were Delft vases and bowls everywhere, decorated with landscapes, flowers, ships and portraits.

Philips

The Philips company of Eindhoven is one of the most familiar names in the field of audio and visual technology. When it started in 1892 the firm produced carbon-filament lamps, but since the Second World War its research department (left) has made numerous technological breakthroughs such as the compact cassette, the video recorder, the compact disc and, more recently, the interactive CD-i system. Today, it is also a major producer of optical communications systems, medical technology, personal electronics and domestic appliances.

Tulip flowers are only left to stand for 10 days to maintain nutrients in the soil.

Tulips

The Netherlands, known as the florist of Europe, exports more flowers than the rest of the world combined. The tulip, which probably came from China originally, now attracts thousands of tourists to the famous tulip fields between Leiden and Haarlem (left). Modern techniques, such as growing cuttings in test tubes, are increasingly common. With this method, up to 1 million disease-free seedlings a year can be grown from a single healthy plant.

LUXEMBOURG

Luxembourg is an independent sovereign state. In the north of the country are the beautiful Ardennes hills, and to the east is the grape-growing Moselle valley. The south is mainly rolling farmland although the old mining region is also here. About a third of the country is forested. Thanks to the wealth created by industry and finance, Luxembourg has one of the highest standards of living in Europe. Its name comes from Anglo-Saxon, and means "little fortress".

Country

The northern part of Luxembourg, known as the Osling, consists of forested hills, meandering rivers and narrow valleys. The Gutland in the south (right) is a more gentle landscape of woodland, lush meadows, and vineyards. Ruined castles and charming villages dot the countryside.

Luxembourg city

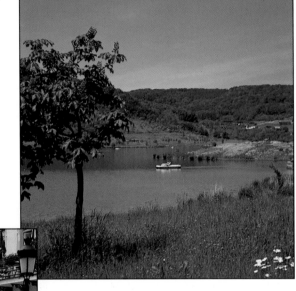

Luxembourg's capital

Luxembourg city was founded by the Romans, as its dramatic situation over the gorges of the Alzette and Pétrusse rivers made it easy to defend. The fortress was destroyed in 1554 by a gunpowder explosion. Today, Luxembourg is a peaceful city of café-lined streets and picturesque parks.

Three languages

As a tiny country, Luxembourg has long understood the need to communicate with its neighbours. As a result, the people of Luxembourg commonly speak at least three languages. Letzeburgesch is the most common everyday language, French is used in most primary schools and German in most secondary schools. Newspapers are in German, and French is used in parliament. Many people speak English fluently too.

Grand Duchy

Luxembourg was established as an independent state in 963. The Duchy of Luxembourg was established in 1354. The title of grand duke is hereditary, its holders belonging to the House of Nassau. Like Belgium, Luxembourg spent many centuries under the control of France, Spain and Austria. In 1815, it became part of the Netherlands, then in 1830 declared its independence. During both world wars, it was occupied by the Germans.

Euros

Food and drink

Farmers in the Bon Pays, or Gutland, region grow barley, oats, potatoes and wheat. On the pasture land, there are large herds of cattle and sheep. Pork is a favourite food, in dishes such as Treipen (black pudding), smoked pork with broad beans, and Ardennes ham. Kachkeis is one of several local cheeses and is often eaten with fruit or grain liqueurs. Beer and white wine from the Moselle valley are popular too.

Luxembourg's high standard of living comes from its financial sector and thriving iron and steel industry. Because of its favourable laws governing banking secrecy and taxation, it is home to more than 260 banks, including the European Investment Bank. It has a very comprehensive welfare system that redistributes over half of government income, and unemployment and inflation are low. Education is compulsory from the ages of 6 to 15, and at 12 children go either to secondary schools or technical colleges.

Redouté (1759-1840)

Born in St Hubert in the Ardennes, Pierre-Joseph Redouté began at the age of 13 a career that was to make him the most influential botanical artist of all time. In Paris he worked for Josephine Bonaparte, creating over 600 vellum drawings that are still studied today.

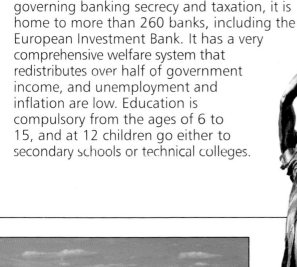

An independent spirit

The people of Luxembourg are independent and content, as expressed in the line from their national anthem *Ons Hemecht* (Our Homeland) which runs *Mir welle bleiwe wat mir sin*, and means "We want to remain what we are". Luxembourg is sometimes seen as a model for a future Europe – a truly cosmopolitan place that has maintained its individuality.

TODAY AND TOMORROW

Home to many important world and European organisations, the Benelux countries are well placed to take advantage of European union. As small countries with a history of foreign interference, they are used to dealing with their neighbours and adapting quickly to changing needs. Though language differences will continue to create tension, the fiercely independent cultures and healthy economies of all three countries will ensure that their influence continues to be felt across the globe.

Centre of power

The Benelux countries manage to exert such a strong influence worldwide partly because they are home to so many important international organisations. The World Trade Centre is in Rotterdam (top of page), NATO (North Atlantic Treaty Organisation) and the European Parliament are in Brussels, and the European Court of Justice and other European Union buildings (above right) are situated in Luxembourg city.

The European Union
Under the Treaty of Maastricht, EU member countries have agreed to new levels of co-operation on money and social matters.

Flag of the European Union

United Nations
The Benelux countries are founder members of the United Nations, set up to maintain peace and security and to solve members' social and economic problems.

Maastricht
The Benelux countries are fervent pro-Europeans, and well understand the advantages of working together with their neighbours. The Maastricht Treaty, signed in 1992 in the Dutch city of that name, committed the member nations of the European Union to work towards greater unity in the future, and gave increased powers to the European Parliament (right) in Brussels.

The European Parliament

The liberal tradition
The Netherlands has a long tradition of liberalism and tolerance, stretching back to the 16th century. Also influenced by the youthful counterculture of the 60s, the Dutch believe that a relaxed, open attitude towards drugs reduces abuse – there are even "smoking" cafés for soft-drug users. This is all part of a general live-and-let-live attitude. The Dutch have also had more success than other nations in controlling hard drugs.

Tourism

Tourism is an important sector of the economy in the Benelux countries. The canals and islands of the Netherlands, the medieval cities of Belgium, and the spectacular forests and river valleys of Luxembourg provide a variety unmatched in such a small area anywhere else in Europe. All these attractions are easily reached by excellent roads, railways and rivers.

The Enkhuizen Zuider Zee Museum in the Netherlands.

NATO

The Benelux countries signed the North Atlantic Treaty in 1949, which stated that an attack against any member would be considered an attack against all members.

ESA

Belgium and the Netherlands are both members of the European Space Agency, established to develop a space programme in Europe.

The struggle against the sea

The Dutch and the Belgians of Flanders have centuries of experience in the fight against the sea. Although their expertise has produced some of the most ingenious engineering solutions for holding back the sea and turning the water into land, they now face another problem. Global warming is threatening to increase the temperature of the world, and to melt some of the ice at the polar caps. If the sea level rises by only a couple of metres, then the area below sea level in the Netherlands, which is home to 60 per cent of the population, may be under threat.

In spite of centuries of foreign rule, Belgium, the Netherlands and Luxembourg have each carved a unique identity for themselves. Since the Second World War their economic union has allowed them to establish economic stability and a good standard of living – a solid platform for future prosperity.

FACTS AND FIGURES

THE NETHERLANDS

Name: Koninkrijk der Nederlanden (Kingdom of the Netherlands)

Capital: Amsterdam

National anthem: *Wilhelmus van Nassouwe* ("William of Nassau")

Official language: Dutch; in the province of Friesland, Friesian is also used as an official language.

Currency: The euro replaced the guilder in 2002

Population: 16,150,000

Population density: 463 persons per sq km

Distribution: 89% urban, 11% rural

BELGIUM

Name: Royaume de Belgique (in French) or Koninkrijk België (in Flemish

Capital: Brussels

National anthem: *La Brabançonne* ("The Brabant Song")

Official languages: Flemish (form of Dutch), French and German.

Currency: As of 2002, the euro, previously the Belgian franc

Population: 10,289,000

Population density: 334 persons per sq km

LUXEMBOURG

Name: Grand-Duché de Luxembourg

Capital: Luxembourg city

National anthem: Ons Hemecht ("Our Homeland")

Official languages: French, German and Letzeburgesch. Letzeburgesch, a dialect of German with many French words, was recognised as an official language in 1984.

Currency: As of 2002, the euro, previously the Luxembourg franc

Population: 454,000

Population density: 164 per sq km

Cheese from Edam

Flowers from province of south Holland

Pottery from Delft

Lace from Ghent

Flax and textile industry, and hop-growing in Flanders

Wallonia, former home of coal and steel industries

Groningen oil fields

Salt from Hengel

Dairy produce and livestock from Dutch sand plains

Flanders, new home of steel industry

Coal from southern uplands

Timber from Ardennes

Steel from Luxembourg

Ethnic groups: Dutch 83%, other 17%, of which 9% are non-western, mainly from former colonies in Indonesia and Surinam.

Religion: Roman Catholic 31%, Protestant 21%, no religious affiliation 40%, Muslim 4.5 %, other 3.6%

Area: 33,938 sq km

Size: north–south 315km, east–west 260km

Highest point: Mount Vaalserberg, 321m above sea level

Lowest point: Prins Alexander Polder, 6.7m below sea level

Ethnic groups: Fleming 58%, Walloon 31%, mixed or other 11%.

Religion: Roman Catholic 88%, Muslim 2.5%, Protestant 1%, other 8.5%

Area: 30,528 sq km

Size: east–west 274km, north–south 225km

Highest point: Botrange mountain, 694m above sea level

Lowest point: Sea level

Ethnic groups: Luxembourger 66%, Portuguese 12%, Italian 5%, French 4%, Belgian 3%, German 2%, other 8%

Religion: Roman Catholic 87%, some Protestants, Jews and Muslims.

Area: 2,586 sq km

Size: north–south 89km, east–west 56km

Highest point: Burgplatz, 559m above sea level

Lowest point: Moselle river, 133m above sea level

THE NETHERLANDS

Coastlines: North Sea to the north west (367km)

Main rivers: Rhine, Maas, Waal and Scheldt

Climate: As Belgium

Location/physical features: Four main regions – The Dunes, 4.5 to 7.5m above sea level, along the entire North Sea coast, mainly sand; The Polders, mostly below sea level and protected by dykes, but most productive farmlands and biggest cities; The Sand Plains in the south-east, less than 30m above sea level, landscape of pine forests and clay soils (near rivers); and Southern Uplands, the highest land region with fertile soils where much fruit is grown in orchards.

Crop production: (tonnes) Potatoes 7.3 million, sugar beets 7.6 million, wheat 1.2 million, apples 570,000, tomatoes 525,000, cucumbers 500,000, onions 453,000, barley 218,000.

Livestock: Pigs 14 million, cattle 4.5 million, sheep 1.7 million.

Main industries: Agro-industries, metal and engineering products (below right); electrical machinery and equipment; chemicals; petroleum; construction; microelectronics.

Main imports:
Machinery and transport; food and live animals; chemicals; foodstuffs; clothing; minerals and fuels.

Main exports:
Machinery and transport; basic manufactures; chemicals; food and live animals; minerals and fuels.

BELGIUM

Coastlines: North Sea to the north west (63km)

Main rivers: Scheldt, Sambre, Meuse

Climate: Moderate marine climate, marked by mild winters with little frost, fairly cool summers and a good deal of wind and rain.

Location/physical features: There are four main land regions – the coastal and interior lowlands in the north protected from the sea by dykes; the Kempenland in the north-east (traditionally covered in birch forests), the central low plateaus with the country's best agricultural land and large cities such as Brussels; and the Ardennes, an area of forest-covered hills separated by winding rivers.

Crop production: (tonnes) Sugar beets 5.2 million, potatoes 2.5 million, wheat 1.9 million, barley 435,500. Other important crops include fruits, tomatoes and flax.

Livestock: Pigs 7 million, cattle 3 million, sheep 161,000, horses 24,000.

Main industries: Engineering and metal products; processed food and beverages; chemicals; basic metals; textiles; glass; plastics; petroleum; coal.

Main imports:
Machinery and transport; basic manufactures; chemicals and related products; food and live animals; diamonds; minerals and fuels.

Main exports:
Machinery and transportation equipment; chemicals; diamonds; metals; foodstuffs.

LUXEMBOURG

Coastlines: Luxembourg has no coastline.

Main rivers: Moselle, Sure, Alzette

Climate: As Belgium

Location/physical features: Luxembourg is divided into two regions: Osling in the north of the country is a wooded, hilly region of great natural beauty; Gutland in the south is pastureland.

Crop production: (tonnes) Barley 63,300, wheat 52,800, potatoes 22,800, rye 16,800, oats 11,800, sugar beets 10,400, apples 5,600.

Livestock:
Cattle 214,000, pigs 76,600.

Main industries:
Banking; iron and steel; food processing; chemicals; metal products; engineering; tyres; glass; aluminium.

Main imports:
Minerals; metals; foodstuffs; quality consumer goods.

Major import sources:
Belgium 30%, Germany 23%, France 13%, The Netherlands 5%, Taiwan 7%.

Main exports:
Machinery and equipment; steel products; chemicals; rubber products; plastics; textiles; gas.

Major export destinations:
Germany 24%, France 21%, Belgium 11%, UK 9%, Italy 6%, Spain 5%, Netherlands 4%.

ECONOMY

The GDP (gross domestic product) is the amount of goods and services produced within a country. By dividing the GDP by the population a *per capita* result is reached.

Figures shown are the GDP per capita in the year 2002 (GDP's are shown in U.S. dollars).

Netherlands	27,011
Belgium	28,964
Luxembourg	44,586
U.S.	35,935
Germany	26,234
U.K.	25,427

FAMOUS FACES

WRITERS

SCIENTISTS

Desiderius Erasmus (1466-1536, right), born in Rotterdam, was one of the most influential figures in the Renaissance. His hostility to the Catholic Church helped pave the way for the Reformation.

Georges Simenon (1903-89). See page 14.

Benedictus de Spinoza (1632-77), born in Amsterdam, was a Dutch-Jewish philosopher, and one of the greatest thinkers of the 17th century.

Anne Frank (1929-45, left). See page 9.

Count Maurice Maeterlinck (1862-1949), born in Ghent, was a Belgian dramatist. He wrote many philosophical works, and won the Nobel Prize for literature in 1911.

Hergé (Georges Remi, 1907-83). See page 14.

Anton van Leeuwenhoek (1632-1723, right). Born at Delft, he became a famous microscopist, and made important discoveries concerning the circulation of the blood, blood corpuscles and the skin.

Leo Baekeland (1863-1944). See page 17.

Abbé Lemaître (1894-1966). See page 17.

Hugo de Vries (1848-1935) was a Dutch botanist, born at Haarlem, who developed theories of plant genetics and evolutionary theory.

Andreas Vesalius (1514-64, left) was a Belgian anatomist, born in Brussels. He advanced studies of biology and anatomy with his descriptions of bones and the nervous system, discovered by dissecting cadavers. The Inquisition sentenced him to death for "body snatching", later commuted to a pilgrimage to Jerusalem.

Christiaan Huygens (1629-93, right), born in The Hague, was an important physicist. Amongst his many achievements and discoveries, he developed the pendulum clock, following Galileo's theory, and discovered the rings of Saturn.

Marie Eugene Dubois (1858-1940). Born at Eijsden, Holland, he discovered "Java man", which he claimed was the missing link between apes and man. After initial ridicule, his views became accepted, although by then, Dubois was convinced the bones were of a giant gibbon.

MUSICIANS

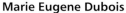

Roland de Lassus (1532-94) was a Flemish composer. He trained in Italy, and joined the court of Duke Albrecht of Bavaria. His madrigals and chansons made him famous throughout Europe.

Cesar Auguste Franck (1822-90, right), a composer, was born in Liège into a German family. He began as a pianist, and his compositions were originally considered too daring, until a number of established musicians, including Liszt, championed him. His reputation is based on a few pieces written after the age of 50.

Adolphe Sax (1814-94, below left). See page 15.

Jacques Brel (1929-78). Singer and songwriter, born in Brussels but settled in Paris. Known for his lyrical sharpness and passionate voice, his songs include *Ne Me Quitte Pas*, *Mathilde* and *Amsterdam*.

ENCORE!

Gerardus Mercator (1512-94, below left), was a Flemish geographer and map-maker. The Mercator projection is still used for nautical charts. He published the first part of a world "Atlas", the first time the term had been used. The book was so-called because it had Atlas holding a globe on the cover.

Audrey Hepburn (1929-93, right). Born in Brussels to Dutch and British parents, Audrey Hepburn's real name was Edda Hepburn van Heemstra. She trained as a ballet dancer but found fame as an actress, winning an Oscar for her role in *Roman Holiday* (1953).

PAINTERS

Belgium and the Netherlands have produced many fine artists. Jan van Eyck (1385-1441) was the first to use native landscapes as backdrops for biblical scenes. Hieronymous Bosch (1460-1516) painted gruesome visions of hell and hideous beasts. Peter Paul Rubens (1577-1640, below right), travelled to Italy to study the Renaissance artists, and became the most influential artist of the 17th century. His dynamic pictures and energetic figures caused a sensation. As the Netherlands grew rich in the 17th century, merchants commissioned many paintings. The Renaissance brought changes in painting techniques, and the way the human body was painted became more important than the subject.

(Above) *The Garden of Earthly Delights* by Hieronymous Bosch.

After the Reformation in the Netherlands, the Calvinists forbade religious paintings. Therefore artists painted different subjects, such as scenes from everyday life, landscapes, and still lifes.

One of the most original artists was Rembrandt van Rijn (1606-69, above left). As a young man, he was extremely popular, but his later pictures upset his patrons and he died bitter and bankrupt.

Vermeer (1632-75) was known for the peace and intimacy of his pictures, and the trademark of Frans Hals (1585-1666) was his ability to capture a facial expression.

As the prosperity of the Netherlands waned in the 18th century, so did the quality and originality of its art. The 19th century produced Vincent Van Gogh (left), although he didn't receive recognition until after his death. Popular 20th century artists were Piet Mondrian (1872-1944), with his celebrated grids, and Belgian René Magritte (1898-1967), who depicted surrealistic, dream-like scenes of strange objects in unlikely places.

(Below) *Man in Armour* by Rembrandt van Rijn.

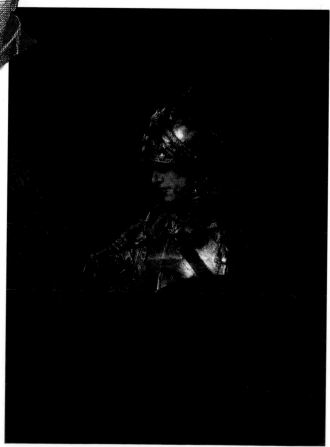

INDEX